IT'S NEVER TOO LATE

Anonymous

WESTBOW
PRESS®
A DIVISION OF THOMAS NELSON
& ZONDERVAN

WestBow Press books may be ordered through
booksellers or by contacting:

WestBow Press
A Division of Thomas Nelson & Zondervan
1663 Liberty Drive
Bloomington, IN 47403
www.westbowpress.com
844-714-3454

ISBN: 978-1-9736-2093-8 (sc)
ISBN: 978-1-9736-2092-1 (e)

Library of Congress Control Number: 2018902388

Print information available on the last page.

WestBow Press rev. date: 12/28/2021

Contents

Foreword

Some of my memories are related to the title of this book: I know that its too late on a number of important life issues: For example, I feel like I missed out on having a loving relationship with my earthly father, and of course it's too late. He died many years ago. There were many times he was not there when I needed him, particularly in the teenage years. It's also too late for my wife and I to bring up our children now that they are grown and on their own. It's too late for my wife and I to relive the early years of our marriage, many of which were painful. We were so young and wounded, and certainly not following Biblical principles concerning marriage. So, until recently, I felt it was too late to bring God glory with the remaining years I have left on planet earth. However, the Holy Spirit has convicted me that at age 73, it's never too late for God to redeem the years the crawling locust, the swarming locust, the hopping locust, the stripping locust have stolen from the two of us, and that there are Christian men and women of all ages who would benefit from many of our experiences. It is our prayer that what God has shown us will be a testimony to His faithfulness.

A small caveat: all of what follows is not meant to be a formula. If there was such a formula that could "fix" all our issues, we would want to memorize it and become very much like the Galatia Christians. Overcoming our fleshly desires is a daily, hour-by-hour, life long process. Adapt and put into practice whatever works for you in order to achieve success as you move forward. What follows is meant to recalibrate your heart.

1

It's Never Too Late
.....TO BEGIN AGAIN

If you, as a Christian, have been worrying and feeling guilty over long past or very recent sins, and been voicing, "How could I have done it" or "I must have been out of my mind,' or you are meditating on an accusatory voice that says you're not good enough and you never will be, then first of all, BEGIN the process of understanding yourself. This may be uncharted waters for you, but you will learn, like Peter, to be a water walker and a mountain mover.

First of all, be assured that you have not lost your salvation. I John 5:13 (AMP) says,

> "I write to you who believe in (adhere to, trust in, and rely on) the name of the Son of God, so that you may know (with settled and absolute knowledge) that you already have life, yes, eternal life."

If you had children, did they keep asking you if they were still one of your children? Did they keep asking you if you still loved them?

Also we read in Ephesians 2:8-9 (NKJV)also says, "For by grace you have been saved through faith and that not of yourselves; it is the gift of God not of works, lest anyone should boast." God gave you your salvation, and He is not about to take the gift back.

So let's go a step further: Here's what God's Word says about you and me.

"We naturally love to do evil things that are just the opposite from the things that the Holy Spirit tells us to do; and the good things we want to do when the Spirit has His way with us are just the opposite of our natural desires. These two forces within you (the Holy Spirit and the your evil nature) are constantly fighting each other to win control over us and our wishes are NEVER free from their pressures". (Gal. 5:17-NLT)

So don't be shocked over your behavior; you're human and although He will correct us for our behavior, God does not keep on berating us over and over again for the same sin. The evil one does. i.e. if you raised children, did you keep spanking them over and over again for the same misbehavior?

It's Never Too Late
.....FOR THE GOOD NEWS

"It's never too late – God's personal message to you and me as believers is,

> "Come back to me and really mean it; come fasting and weeping, sorry for your sins; Change your life, not just your clothes; Come back to God, your God; And here's why: God is kind and merciful; He takes a deep breath, puts up with a lot.

This most patient God, extravagant in love, always ready to cancel catastrophe. Come back to God and really mean it" (Joel 2:12-Msg). Obviously, "come back" implies that you left.

II Chronicles 7:14 says:

"If My people who are called by My name, shall humble themselves, pray, seek, crave and require of necessity My face and turn from their wicked ways, then will I hear from heaven, forgive their sin and heal their land." (AMPL);you and I are one of His people, we acknowledge our sinful ways (not easily done or admitted), and we have turned away from them.

Perhaps you may think you no longer sin as a believer. However, the Bible makes this very clear in the flowing verses:

"All have sinned and are falling short of the honor and glory which God bestows (Rom. 3:23 (AMP)

"There is none righteous, no, not one" (Rom. 3:10;NKJV) and also,

"No one anywhere has kept on doing what is right ; not one"(Rom. 3:12;TLB)

In other words, we could not trust one day of our life to get us into Heaven.

God's promises: "For Christ also suffered once to death in the flesh but made alive by the Spirit. 1 Peter 3:18(KJV)

"But if we are really living in the light, as He is in the light, we have (true, unbroken) fellowship with one another, and the blood of Jesus Christ His Son cleanses (removes) us from all sin and guilt (keeps us cleansed from sin in all its forms and manifestations). If we say we have no sin (refusing to admit that we are sinners), we delude and lead ourselves astray and the truth is not in us (does not dwell in our hearts). If we admit that we have sinned and confess our sins, He is faithful and just and will forgive our sins and continuously cleanse us from all unrighteousness."

(1 John:1:7-9;AMP).

Several songs come to mind as I think about the sacrifice that Jesus made on the cross to pay my debt of sin. The first one I love to sing is, "What can wash away my sin? Only the blood of Jesus" and "There is power in the blood of Jesus, wonder working power in the blood of the lamb" Another one that has stayed in my mind for years is, "Say goodbye to every sin; You love me even though I don't deserve it."

Part of confessing involves humbling yourself before God. This is because we are flushing out our pride, which is the most basic of deadly sins. Pride leads to every other vice. It is a complete anti-God state of mind. On the other hand, humility is the foundation to all other virtues. Humility allows us a grace of receptivity and allows us the freedom to take the growth steps we need. God gives grace to the humble, and that's why humility is a medicine to be taken daily, drop-by-drop.

But humility can also be carried to the point of being spoiled by pride. It would be as if someone said, "Have you seen my book on humility: It's really quite good!"

Note: Don't dwell on thinking about your sin behaviors. Just confess them and apply the blood of Jesus. I will share more about the importance of proactively doing this, continually during the day, later in Chapter 3. So when your sin pops ups again, remind yourself that it's confessed to God and you have applied the blood of Jesus to it.

We have all had issues that tempted us from time to time. As we recall them, we remember some we dealt with successfully. Others we were not so successful.

For example, an issue that I had the most difficulty dealing with was a sexual temptation as a teenager. The pleasure I received became a strong hold without me realizing it; I really didn't think there was anything wrong; as a matter of fact, when I first heard it was a sin, I thought it was way too judgmental and it was just a natural release. Then I developed an addiction to pornography, reading the letters to Penthouse magazine to be specific. My rationale was that this just helped me develop my sex drive. I thank God I didn't go any further. i.e. viewing tapes or the internet. The above is also an example of how one thing leads to another. This is an example of how the evil one establishes strongholds in our mind. We need to be so diligent about what we look at and listen to.

Many Christian men and women deal with sexual sin in one way or another but have also found deliverance and healing. And before you judge anyone who has committed sexual sins too harshly, remember what Jesus said,:

> "But I say: Anyone who even looks
> at a women with lust in his eye has
> already committed adultery with her
> in his heart." (Matthew 5:28-NLT);

Consistent surveys show that at least 60% of men and 40% of women have committed adultery. (This does not make it right or justify it!!!)See Esther

Perel's book "In defense of adulterers." But Jesus also said, to the ones who had caught the woman in adultery: " He who is without sin among you, let him throw a stone at her first." (John 8:7 NKJV)

But, then comes the daily pressing convictions, the voices inside my head, the guilt i.e. I can't say I never sinned. I feel like David, when he says, "My sin is ever before me".

Are these voices from the Lord or the evil one or are they just self voices which come from the habit of believing the worst about yourself?; Remember we hear "voices" on multiple levels. Are you able to watch TV and listen to someone speak to you at the same time? Can you drive your car, speak to a passenger, and listen to the radio? Of course, you can. So remember to combat the voices on all the different levels that come at you.

So what is the good news? Since the conviction over past sins is something I deal with on a daily basis, what should I do about it?

3

It's Never Too Late
...FOR MORE GOOD NEWS

OK; here is what to do and it may not be easy: The rewiring or the renewing of your mind which is like reprogramming.

As I have stated before, it has to be daily, minute by minute and hourly talking to your inner self like David did (read all of Psalm 51)

Every day, before you get out of bed, talk to God in the name of Jesus Christ. God, Himself, tore down the curtain that separates us from Him;.

You do this because every morning negative, accusatory thoughts will rush at you like wild dogs, and you can not ignore them.

Invoke the blood of Jesus Christ over your mind many times during the day. It helps me to picture the Sherman Williams ad showing a can of paint being tipped over, covering the earth. The blood of Jesus is covering my mind with the same impenetrable covering. This step is probably the most important one to apply because Satan and all his demons do not want to hear about the blood of Jesus. When you say this out loud or even whisper it, they will flee even before you have it out of your mouth. "Resist the evil one and he will flee from you" (I Peter 5:9) Satan knows who Jesus is, but he doesn't want to hear about the blood of Jesus.

The importance of invoking the blood of Jesus was brought home to me a number of years ago: As I was walking along our garden talking with the Lord, I happened to look up, and clear as day, on a telephone wire, sat what appeared to me to be two hooded vulture-like creatures looking down at me. Anger and fear came over me and I started yelling at them, They just kept on looking at me, but as soon as I pointed my finger at them, and said," I invoke the rich red living blood of Jesus Christ" they vanished. They actually vanished before I could complete the word "blood"

Other ways we can have conversations with God include the "Lord's Prayer". As this prayer models for us, Jesus reminds us that God exists in heaven, and He hears and listens to us. It takes 21 seconds to pray this prayer, so pray it many times throughout times a day. Mark Rutland has an entire book on this entitled, "21 Seconds to Change your World".

Use your prayer language/pray in tongues. We are taught that when we do so, we are talking to God and the evil one does not know what you are saying. It is also helpful in edifying yourself.

(see I Corinthians 14). If you don't have a prayer language, ask Him to give you one. He gives good gifts to them that ask. (see James 1:5-8)

There are lots of encouraging scriptures to ourselves. Examples can be found in the Old and New Testament;

> "Who forgives every one of) all your iniquities, who heals (each one of) all your diseases, Who redeems your life from the pit and corruption, Who beautifies, dignifies and crowns me with loving-kindness and tender mercy" (Psalm 103:3-4 AMP))

> "His love for me is unconditional." (Read Corinthians 13) and

> "No weapon formed against you shall prosper…" (Isaiah 54:17 AMP)

Join the angels and people in Heaven by praising and worshiping Him; "I love you Lord and I raise my voice to worship you for when your eyes are on this child, your grace abounds to me."

Breath deeply and often during the day. This is a practical suggestion, and experts are increasingly agreeing that simple breathing exercises provide immediate benefits from stress. To begin right away, get in a comfortable position, breath 4-8 times from your stomach through your nose. Do this 1-3 times a day. Google "Deep breathing" for more information.

Every day all of us go through a cycle i.e. our up's and down's. Define yourself: are you a morning, afternoon, or night person. As an example, I seem to be a two cycle person: I wake up and says "This is the day the Lord has made" and I thank the Lord for bringing me safely through the night. Then around 10 AM, I feel myself starting to go down (so I eat a snack). After lunch which includes a piece of chocolate, I feel better. Later on I go through another cycle. You and I are brighter and more attentive during the peaks; conversely, during a down period, we are more easily influenced by the negative voices in our head or from the outside, like a phone call or an email. When you feel an attack coming on, go into counter attack mode. which means you come at the enemy with overwhelming force. (Anyone in the military understands this.) Like quoting appropriate versus from the Bible, reminding yourself who you are (You're not the same person you used to be), and asking God for help. He doesn't mind hearing from you. It's His battle, you are in it. Also when you feel like there is a war going on in your head, it's like an island experiencing a hurricane, hang on to the coconut tree till the storm passes. In other words, do your best to resist the evil one, and he will eventually leave you.

Don't feel guilty about taking doctor prescribed

medication. Remind yourself that you are trusting the medicine and also God's Word to heal your soul and body.

Pray for each other. I have found that sharing my needs and heart's desires with other trusted believers is extremely freeing. "again I say to you that if two of you agree on earth concerning anything that they ask, it will be done for them by My Father in heaven. For where two or three are gathered together I My name, I am there in the midst of them.' (Matthew 18:19-20 NKJV)

Each day align your feelings with the Word of God. Circumstances can mislead us. Our feelings are subjective, so the Word should be what we look to for guidance. Our feelings should be the caboose of our train.

Re-pray whatever part of the "sinner's prayer" that applies to you. You might begin with: "Father God, the name of Jesus, I think I may have never prayed this prayer with a sincere heart and really meant it …..." Or possibly "Father God, in the name of Jesus, I have sinned against you and my self, in thought, word, and deed and I confess and repent of ……"

Or "I ask you to heal any vestige of bitter hurt in me and by the power of The Holy Spirit bring to my mind and heart, now and forever, only those memories which serve to restore, refresh, and delight., through Jesus Christ, your son, my Lord.

Or "the sinner's prayer:" "Thank you, God, for loving me and sending your son to die for my sins. I sincerely repent of my sins and receive Christ as my personal savior, Now, as your child, I turn over my entire life over to you. Amen"

Beware: Be on guard; see yourself as a sentry walking back and forth on the castle of your mind. The demonic influences are like the old TV show called "Candid Camera:" The producers hid a camera in order to catch a person doing something silly. At the end of each show, the announcer would say, "Be careful because when you least expect it, you too may hear, "Smile, you're on Candid Camera"

Well, the evil one takes great delight in reminding us of our sin, when we least expect it.

Don't overanalyze your self or your situation. This has been called paralysis by analysis. Striving for perfection will cause this. It's all right to try for excellence, but not perfection. We can never achieve perfection. I have played tennis for many years and I am most miserable when I try for perfection. It makes me want to smash the racket and curse. Thankfully, I have been delivered from this attitude, although hitting the perfect shot is SO satisfying!

You will probably have to end certain friendships. This is not because you have become better than others. The Word says "Bad company corrupts good character."

Say over and over "Jesus loves me; this I

know; for the Bible tells me so; little ones to Him belong,He is strong, when I am weak" Believe that God loves you more than you love yourself.

As a result of realizing that it's never too late, you and I can now practice our God- given ministry to many people.: Where it is appropriate, you and I can say, "I know what you are going through. I have dealt with and deal with the same thing."

If you have put into practice the above, and your old tapes start to remind you "what about what you just did this morning... or yesterday? This is the crucial point at which you speak the Word of Truth over the situation and do not give over any ground to the enemy.

Say to yourself that all of the above is a big fat lie OR it is the truth. And, course it's the truth:

We are like the woman at Jacob's well (see John 4) or like the woman caught in adultery: Jesus said to her " I do not condemn you. Go on your way and from now on sin no more."(John 8:11 NKJV); We are also like the prodigal son; The father did not turn him away, saying your sins are too great and you are not welcome to come home He did just the opposite.

So, continue your conversation with yourself: For example, say," I no longer want to be forgiven so I can go and sin some more." Paul deals with this attitude in Romans 6:1 "What shall we say to all this? Are we to remain in sin in order that God's grace, His favor and mercy, may multiply and over flow? "Certainly not!" It's the change in desire and attitude he is looking for, not perfection.

There are people in your past you need to forgive. I can say that with certainty because there is no one on the planet that does not need to forgive. Forgiveness is defined as to pardon, to cancel, to excuse, or to grant. We need to forgive, first of all, ourselves and then people in our past: start with yourself: you know what you have done to wound others. Satan will remind you daily. They are sins that haunt you; This forgiveness starts with admitting to yourself what it is that you are harboring, and then visualizing yourself letting yourself out of prison. You then proceed to do the same to all the others. It's not easy, but you at least begin the process.

I began by dredging up each one of the situations in which I was at fault and applying the blood of Jesus, and forgiving myself. I then made up a list of the people I needed to forgive; It included my wife, mother and father, children, brothers, former friends and coworkers etc.

An example is my mother: she was very strict (raising 5 boys), and after I left home, I realized I had a lot of anger toward her. A conference I attended recommended that we telephone any one who we needed to forgive, and when I called her, she instantly forgave me, and a healing began between the two of us.

Remember the story Jesus told of the King who wanted to settle accounts with his servants: He forgave the one who owed him 10,000 talents, but when that same servant was asked by a fellow servant to forgive 100 denarii, he refused. When the King found out about this, he had the servant thrown in jail. Until we forgive, we are as guilty as the first servant. But by beginning the process of forgiving, you release yourself from the debt of unforgiveness. (See Matthew 18:23-35)

When you sinned as a Christian in the area in which you have had a weakness, the evil one tempted you and enticed you because you were a "easy value target" for him, and now that you are a "high value target".

> 2 Corinthians 11:3 says, "...even as the serpent beguiled Eve by his cunning, so your mind may be corrupted and seduced from a

wholehearted and sincere and pure devotion to Christ." (AMP)

You join many people in the Bible such as the following.

"Paul who said "....of sinners, I AM chief"(1 Timothy 1:15 NKJV)

I thought he should have said, "I used to be before I met Jesus on the road to Damascus..

Adam and Eve: She is a good example of what happens to us when we listen to and dialogue with satan.

David committed murder and adultery.

Noah who had relations with his daughters.

Peter, who used curse words (see the original Greek text) when he denied Jesus three times. (Peter began to place a curse on himself and swear, 'I don't know the man' Matt. 26:74. NKJV)

Sampson who, as a married man, pursued an improper relationship with another woman.

The churches mentioned in the Book of the Revelation.

Read what Haratio Spafford,the man who wrote the much loved hymn, "It is Well with my Soul" said about himself: "My sin not in part but the whole is nailed to the cross, and I bear it no more"

Here's some more good news: Your sin has become your salvation and deliverance: You know the story of Joseph. He was sold into slavery by his brothers, but ended up second to Pharaoh and prepared the country for the famine that occurred. His brothers came begging for grain which he gave to them. But, more importantly, their sin became their salvation. They were spared from dying of hunger but the greatest gift was being reconciled with their brother. I understood this concept for years, but I never personalized it.

Maybe at this point you say "Okay, what should I do next?

Stay in the Word and focus on what Jesus said,"If you remaining me and I in you, you will bear much fruit; apart from me you can do nothing (John 15:5-NIV)

It's Never Too Late
.......ENCOURAGEMENT

All of us need to be given confidence or have our hopes lifted every day. It can happen a variety of ways and among them are the Bible, encouraging words from loved ones and inspirational books. Below are numerous bullet points and personal stories meant to do just that:

Phillipians 1:6 says "He who began a good work in you...(that's you!) He will complete it until the day of Jesus Christ" (NKJV) You are under construction for the rest of your life. Failure is like getting tackled behind the line of scrimmage: you pick yourself up and get back in the game. Don't be afraid of failure. Psalm 138:8 "The Lord will perfect that which concerns me."(NKJV)

Romans 10 says: "Because if you acknowledge with your mouth (your confession is voice activated!) and believe in your heart (belief releases a blessing) that God raised Him from the dead…"(NKJV)

It begins with saying "Yes" to the one who died for you; you've done that! Remember Romans 3:25 says, "whom God set forth as a propitiation by His blood through faith to demonstrate His righteousness, because in His forbearance God had passed over the sins that were previously committed." (NKJV) Propitiation means the appeasement of divine wrath by a sacrificial offering. Christ bore the wrath that we deserve, and it's not stored up for us!

We have been rescued from the jaws of the evil one again and again:

> If you feel like the evil one has you in his jaws, see Amos 3:12
>
> "Thus says the Lord: as a shepherd rescues out of the mouth of the lion (the evil one) two legs or a piece of ear,(of a sheep) "so shall the children of Israel be rescued." (AMP). You and I have been saved i.e. personalize this verse. Hasn't He rescued us many times?

A personal experience about my being rescued from forty years ago. It happened while traveling Latin America as a businessman. On this particular trip, among other countries, I went to Panama; I had heard about marijuana called "Panama Red" and was looking forward to the experience of enlightenment it was supposedly going to give me. Boy, how wrong I was: I went to downtown Panama City and found a taxi cab driver who shared with me a cigar of Panama Red. Within minutes, I was high as a kite; He offered to take me to a place where I could buy some more; when we approached the shanty part of town, he told me to get out, wait for him, and he would be back with the goods taking the $20 I gave him. Well, as you might suspect, he never came back, I found myself in the middle of a row of grass and plywood shacks on both sides of a narrow dirty street, high as a kite, and trying to figure out how to get back to the center of town with the purpose of finding the taxi cab driver who had fleeced me A gas station just happened to be near by, and I hitched a ride to the center of town to look for the taxi driver. There I was met by 3 local thugs who offered to "help" me. As they surrounded me, a taxi just happened to come by. I flagged it down, jumped in, and was taken back to the hotel where I crawled in bed shaking over what I had narrowly escaped. As I look back, I can clearly see that the Lord rescued me, even though I didn't have the sense to pray to be rescued.

Because of many other narrow escapes, many of my own causing, I am so grateful for God's constant care, and you get the point: God has rescued you and me more times than we can count and more times we even realize. When we get to Heaven, He might show us where and when He rescued us, In the meantime, be grateful for His many rescues.

In whatever situation you are currently in, God is asking you "Do you trust Me?" If you will trust Him, you will enter into His rest.

Your dominant weakness is being used by God to bring you under the influence of His word.

Remember as you wait, "The end of a thing is better than its beginning" (Ecclesiastes 7:8 NKJV);In other words, your life is not over. He has a plan for the rest of your life; He is restoring what the locust stole.

The evil one will play a soundtrack over and over again in your mind reminding you of your sins. Replace the evil one's soundtrack with your own soundtrack. Worship and praise is a good way to begin.. Hum some of your favorite Christian songs during the day. Then, come up with your own specific game plan. Put it in writing. This is part of renewing your mind. It's not like falling off a log, and it takes time.

Desire realized is sweet to the soul. Your renewed desire is to please Him, to listen to Him, to enjoy crawling up in His lap cuddling with Him and receiving His hugs.

Grace can be defined as God's undeserved divine favor, and it is something all of us should enjoy every day. Relax and let it fall on you morning, noon, and night. For when His eyes are on this child, His grace abounds toward me is a great way to receive it. You are one of His children, get in His lap, and ask Him. The word Abba in the Lord's prayer literally translated means Daddy.

Remind yourself daily that His grace is greater than your sins; no matter what you've done! If we won't believe this, then Jesus didn't die for ALL you sins, and His crucifixion wasn't enough. This absolutely not true: He died for all our sins, past, present, and future. And when He said,"It is finished" it pertains to all of us!

When you find yourself believing the worst about yourself, arrest yourself; rehearse the good things you have done. I have a tendency to think the worst, and it helps me to remind myself that when I have done the wrong thing, I have confessed, repented and corrected my behavior by doing the right thing. It's like apologizing to someone and asking for forgiveness. Give yourself a break.

Like David, we should appeal to the Lord for mercy: "I have trusted in Your mercy." Psalm 13:5 NKJV

"Psalm 18:25: "With the merciful You will show Yourself merciful." (NKJV

"Psalm 23:6:"surely goodness and mercy shall follow me all the days of my life." (NKJV)

"According to your mercy remember me." Psalm 25:10: (NKVJ)

"All the paths of the Lord are mercy…" Psalm 26:11:"(NKJV)

"Redeem me and be merciful to me" Psalm 27:7(NKJV)

"Have mercy also on me…" Psalm:33:22(NKJV)

"I said, 'Lord, be merciful to me."

Psalm 41:4(NKJV)

"Have mercy upon me, O God..."

Psalm 57:1 (NKJV)

Mercy is defined in Webster's as "compassionate rather than severe behavior toward someone i.e. it's a mercy that the doctor arrived in time."

When you become acutely aware of your sins, it is normal to feel grief: There are stages of grief: denial, anger, depression, bargaining and acceptance. One does not necessarily go through one to another. They seem to swirl around and out of nowhere comes a stage that tries to take you down. You can even feel good and then feel bad for feeling good.

5

It's Never Too Late
.....HEALING OF MEMORIES

Healing is defined as becoming well or whole again; to cause painful emotions to no longer be painful; to bring about reconciliation, and this may be the hardest: We all have memories of the past. They are like the baggage we take on a trip, and their names are guilt, loneliness, shame, doubt, fear, despair, addiction, rejection. Some are when we were hurt deeply, and others are when we sinned against another person. Inside the soul part of you (your mind, emotion and will) are all of these. Or put another way, they are in your subconscious, and like termites, they eat away at us. Until we successfully deal with them, they remain diseased.

David understood the need for healing very well,: "My sorrow is continually before me."(Psalm 38:17 NKJV);"My iniquities have overtaken me, so that I am not able to look up ;They are more than the hairs of my head. "(Psalm 40:12 NKJV)

Nehemiah also confessed, "I pray before You, day and night, for the children of Israel Your servants and confess the sins of the children of Israel which we have sinned against you. Both my father's house and I have sinned"(Neh. 1:6b) NKJV)

In order to receive healing for these memories and to rob them of the power they have over us, we begin by asking in prayer to Jesus that He would take us to these memories, holding our hand. and bring them to the surface. Jesus will bring healing, As it says in Psalm 103, "who forgives all your sins and heals all your diseases" As we learn to listen to Him, He will lead you very specifically to what to confess and who to forgive. This will be painful at first, but He wants to make you whole. When they come up (not if), apply the blood of Jesus to them, continually affirming His blood.

When we became saved, Jesus Christ came into our spirit, and we now need to believe that He is radiating up through our mind and emotion. We practice the practice the presence of God in our mind every day, all day. With His help, we are snatching victory out of the jaws of defeat daily, hour by hour.

Prologue

You may wonder when I became a Christian: I was baptized as an infant. At age 7, I received Jesus as my Savior, after Rev. 3;20-21 was explained to me: We were living in Lima, Peru, and a missionary named Ruth who was with the Billy Graham crusade came to live with us. She explained what it meant to ask Jesus to come into your heart, and I did. She then cautioned me to remember to speak with Him every day (which I neglected to do);Later at age 14, I went through confirmation classes in the Episcopal church in Staten Island. I've also had other 'I see the light experiences" at Maranatha Ministries in Paducah, Kentucky, and one time, after the leader explained baptism, He baptized me by immersion in the name of Jesus. I have also been to numerous other retreats and seminars over the years where I have reaffirmed my faith in Jesus.

So, your appropriate question might be: So what happened? Why did you still sin? The answer is covered in lots of the above but the main one is: I compartmentalized my Christian beliefs. They were a part of me, but I didn't practice His presence in my daily walk with Him. I did not fully commit myself to His care. I was like a person going down a river with one leg in one canoe and the other leg in the second canoe. I loved bubble baths, but after I dried off, I went right back to the world. I was afraid of going too far because if I did, I was convinced He would send me to Africa as a missionary, which at the time, was the scariest thing I could think of!

ALL THINGS HAPPEN FOR THE GOOD
TO ALL THOSE WHO LOVE HIM

So, to continue my testimony, I hit bottom, and it was from there that the Lord began my atonement, regeneration and restoration. Isaiah 42:16 leaped off the page to me "I will lead the blind by the ways they have not known, along unfamiliar paths I will guide them; I will turn the darkness into light before them and make the rough places smooth. (LIV)He helped me see that first of all, I was not believer. I was a church goer. Then, after I became a believer, I went back and forth between the old carnal man and the new spiritual man. I really didn't understand that as a believer, I could still sin in many ways, and when I did sin, I sometimes felt bad but never truly repented. I used to tell people that I was trying to get over "something" but then The Holy Spirit impressed on me that I was going to have to stop being passive and be proactive every hour of every day.

He also deepened the illumination of my thinking:

Earlier I mentioned forgiving myself and other human beings in my life. Forgiveness also means forgiving God. This sounds presumptuous, audacious,, sacrilegious but think about it. You've been harboring a mad toward God for something or for many things. Maybe for your physical makeup, your parents, your childhood etc. Pray "Dear Father God, please forgive me for being mad at you, and thank you for patiently waiting for me to arrive at this realization. I humble myself before you and ask you in all sincerity to forgive me."

Also get a copy of the best book on forgiveness: "The Freedom Factor" by Dr. Bruce Wilkinson. The back jacket of the book says that pastors say that more than 80% of their congregations struggle with unforgiveness. That whatever happened to us happened. But the God who made your heart has shown a way past the wounds, back to life and love.

My sin was due to the carnality deep inside of me: selfishness (including instant self-gratification), gluttony, anger, self pity, the vestige of unforgiveness, bitterness, disobedience. But it's all been flushed down the drain.

God does not desire that you commit murder(suicide)! His son was murdered in your place. God's wrath (that you deserve) was placed on Jesus when He hung on the cross. Continue to believe down in your heart that God can do anything all the time, and that The Holy Spirit is your comforter daily, hourly. He will comfort you personally, and He may send a person, a phone call, an email, a book, a stranger, God's word.

You've begun the deeper journey of understanding yourself: It was the soul part of you (your mind and will) that sinned and so your soul needs atonement. Atonement means a covering. Complete atonement is provided for you and me through the blood of Christ.. For with grace came the blood of Jesus which covers all our sins.

After your soul's atonement, you then begin the process of regeneration. The concept of regeneration is the process of passing out of death into life. You and I receive God's Own life into your spirit. The Holy Spirit now rules your spirit which in turn begins the process of gaining control over your soul and through the soul governs your body. Don't confuse position with experience. The beginning of regeneration is the first step in spiritual development.

Now continues the hard part, but be encouraged: You are like a new fruit: you are not fully mature, and there is boundless possibility for growth.

Embrace your past (instead of reliving it with shame.) Embrace means "to accept, seize, to embrace an opportunity, to take in with the eye of understanding." This is easier said than done, so you continually daily practice being proactive. Again, in summary, here's a few "game plan suggestions:"

A-Begin every day by pleading the Blood of Jesus and continue to do so during the day. See by faith His blood sprinkled over your mind. This is the most important weapon you have. Satan and his evil spirits do not want to hear about the Blood of Jesus. If you don't have a revelation about the blood, ask God to illuminate your mind. This is extremely critical.

Call Sid Roth's 800 number and ask for the package on the blood of Christ ;it includes two books and a CD (800-806-6235); get a copy of Benny Hinn's book "The Blood" Call Osterhus Pub. House (1-877-643-4229) and order copies of "The mind under the blood"

B-Open up His word and search for an encouragement. Pray.

C-Worship Him with a CD. Get a copy of Terry Law's book "The power of Praise and Worship"

D-Read a portion of a Christian help book,but remember it's not self help.

E-Remind yourself that you are not who you used to be

F-Relentlessly oppose regression back to the past in your thinking

G-Use your unknown language frequently

The war for the healing of your mind has begun. You yielded ground to the evil one, and you must begin your recovery of that ground. Begin by recalling the best spiritual experience of your life, Allow your mind to dwell on when you got" turned on" Then ask God to forgive you for getting off course. Jesus said it this way to believers in Rev. 2:5: "Remember therefore from where you have fallen; repent and do the first works..."

However, the evil spirits will withstand your attempts to overthrow their strongholds. They will throw all sorts of lies at you: you are too old, too young, too deficience, too tired., it's too late. Their aim is to mislead you in to thinking that your weakness is natural. The powers of darkness will not surrender without a fight to the very end. Say to them, "The things you are saying about me are bold faced lies, and I will not believe them" Like on a battlefield, maintain your position. God desires your mind to be full of light, wisdom, and understanding, with all its imaginations and reasoning purified and bought into perfect obedience to God's will. Don't let yourself be content with little gain!

The war in your mind will be very painful, at times. There will be bad moments of suffering because the powers of darkness will resist. Such a phenomenon is the sign of victory! The enemy feels the pressure and is making his last stand. Exercise patience and hour by hour, day by day a little at a time, you'll gain more and more ground.

Do not cede any new ground to the enemy ;you are on the road to recovery and liberation.

You will eventually arrive at the same conclusion as Job did, "I know that you can do all things" Job 42:2 NIV). He was transformed and received the gift of grace, a gift he did not deserve. You have become a display of God's grace. Think of that!!

By the way, since you have made a sincere commitment, don't think that The Trinity (God, Jesus, and The Holy Spirit) are saying "You got yourself into this mess ;now let us see you get yourself out of it" It's the opposite: They are running to your aid and well timed help will show up each and every day.

It helped me to pray "God, I can't undo the damage I have done to myself and others; But by your grace and through Jesus Christ, help me to reverse the effects of my sins. You have a plan for my life to make me fruitful. Whatever days I have left on the planet, please help me to obey you, to walk in your truth, and to influence others."

Lastly, recite (during the day) the 23rd Psalm (or portions of it) as a reminder of who He is and who you are:

"The Lord is my shepherd (to feed, guide and shield me.) I shall not lack.

He makes me lie down in (fresh, tender) green pastures; He leads me beside the still waters.

He refreshes and restores my life (my self). He leads me in the paths of righteousness (uprightness and right standing with Him – not for my earning it but) for His name's sake.

Yes, though I walk through the (deep, sunless) valley of the shadow of death, I will fear or dread no evil, for you are with me; Your rod (to protect) and your staff (to guide.)They comfort me.

You prepare a table before me in the presence of my enemies. You anoint my head with oil; my (brimming) cup runs over.

Surely only goodness, mercy, and unfailing love shall follow me all the days of my life, and through the length of my days the house of the Lord (and His presence) shall be my dwelling place,"(AMP)

Now the difficult part

You and I begin the journey from our head to our heart which starts by one baby step at a time:

The first step for us is repentance (changing our mind for the better and amending our ways as God directs us), and the second one is surrender/submission (offering ourselves to Him in full surrender every day.)

The next one is to embrace becoming a servant. Ask God that you would like to become one of His servants, a servant of the most gracious and most merciful God.

Next we begin our faith walk like the believers described in Hebrews 11 who were willing to bear the contempt, abuse, and shame born for Christ to be greater than all the wealth in the world. Faith is simple trust and confidence in God without seeing. We are leaving our Egypt behind us.

Then implement and apply the Passover and

the sprinkling of the Blood of Jesus over your mind and heart and over the doorposts of your house. This is critical and needs to be done out loud every day.

Study the beatitudes and embrace them as our road map that will take us in the right direction. Jesus gives us a superior way to live than the 10 Commandments, and He promises the power to do all that He asks of us as we yield to Him daily. His emphasis is our inner heart transformation by His grace. Remember over and over again it's all by Grace, Grace, Grace.

Along with this, He also said for us to love (unconditionally) and forgive each other as many times as He has forgiven us. If you find it difficult to really forgive someone, at lease release them to God. (As many times, over and over again; really meaning it.)

As we sincerely submit, we then endure correction by God Himself. He is dealing with us as one of His children. None of us are exempt, and afterwards, His discipline will yield in us the fruit of righteousness. (Isn't that what you and I are seeking?)

Tidbit: the experts say that in start a new habit, we have to do it at least 20 times in a row before it becomes a natural new habit. Don't be hard on yourself. If you stumble or fall, it's ok; we all do. We've begun a process and it will take time. By the way, we join Abraham, Sarah, David,, Paul, Peter, and lots of others who stumbled along the new way.

Confess our faults to God and to one another so that we may be healed and restored. This means we are on our way to being healed in our mind and heart.

Read Psalm 139 every day: It begins with "Lord, You know everything there is to know about me; You perceive every movement of my heart and soul and you understand my every thought before it even enters my mind." You'll be tempted to debate this in your mind because you have free will, and if you convince yourself that it's not true, what are you left with? So keep on reading the rest of it. It's overwhelming good news!

We have become believers who have come to our right senses like the prodigal son. Won't God come running down the road to meet us and give us a robe of righteousness. It's also says that Angels rejoice over us.

Admit to God, as a believer, you and I have known a lot about God. (We've been to lots of Bible studies) Now we actually know God. Read what Job said, after his trial and after he never received an answer from God.

Begin to praise and worship Him with a grateful heart for coming down in person into your life. For being so patient with you, for waiting for you to finally come to your senses. Remember, no matter what you done, it's never too late.

If you'll do your part, God will do His part as He deems what is best for you. He has a specific plan for you designed perfectly just for you. You are not a cookie cuter. "I know the plans I have for you and they are not to harm you."

Invite Him into your thought life and think to Him. He knows what you are thinking 24/7, so why not talk to Him in your thoughts. This a great way to "pray without ceasing." Who are you listening to and talking to in your thought life?

Start every day reminding yourself that the Blood of Jesus has and is washing away all of your sins (past ,present, and future). Jesus took all of your sins into himself on the cross. He paid your sin debt in full. You can't pay (by a hang dog attitude) a debt that has already been paid!

Do you remember what your mother said when you first wanted to do X,Y or X? She said "I don't care what everyone else is doing; that's not what we do in this family!" Don't drink the kool aid!

"Father God, Abba (Jesus said I could call you Daddy) and He said I could ask You for anything in His name and You would give it to me. So I'm asking for Your help, for Your wisdom and for Your grace. I'm asking with importunity, and please, please, please give me at least a crumb from Your table. Jesus said You would."

Printed in the United States
by Baker & Taylor Publisher Services